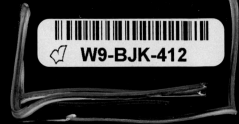

IN THE FOOTSTEPS OF

FRANKENSTEIN

STEVE PARKER

COPPER BEECH BOOKS
BROOKFIELD, CONNECTICUT

© Aladdin Books Ltd 1995

Designed and produced by Aladdin Books Ltd
28 Percy Street
London W1P 0LD

First published in 1995 in the United States by
Copper Beech Books, an imprint of
The Millbrook Press
2 Old New Milford Road
Brookfield, Connecticut 06804

Editor
Jim Pipe
Design
David West Children's
Book Design
Designer
Flick Killerby
Picture Research
Brooks Krikler Picture Research
Illustrators
Susanna Addario, Francesca D'Ottavi – McRae Books, Florence, Italy
Liz Sawyer – Simon Girling & Associates

Printed in Belgium

CIP data is on file at the Library of Congress

ISBN 1-56294-647-1 (lib. bdg.)
1-56294-187-9 (pbk.)

CONTENTS

Mary Shelley's
FRANKENSTEIN

It is a winter day in the late 18th century, and St. Petersburg is thick with snow. Shadowy figures scurry through the streets, keeping their heads low as the cold northern breeze swirls around them. Among these huddled characters, one man stands tall, laughing at the wind. Wouldn't you, if you had just inherited a fortune?

With this money, Robert Walton was pursuing his dream – to travel to the North Pole. No human feet had ever trod this fabled place, where the sun never sets and a wondrous power attracts the needle of the navigator's compass. Some believe that snow and frost are banished there, and that the pole is a region of amazing beauty and wonders.

Walton had spent the last six years preparing for this quest, enduring cold, hunger, and other hardships on whaling expeditions in the northern seas. Now he was heading north, to the port of Archangel, to hire a ship and crew. Throughout his journey, he wrote to his sister, Margaret Saville, who was back in England. This is his story – a tale of discovery, obsession, and monstrous fear...

To Mrs Margaret Saville
England

St Petersburg, Dec. 11th, 17–

Dear Margaret,

You will rejoice that no disaster has accompanied the commencement of an enterprise which you have regarded with such evil forebodings. I arrived here yesterday; and my first task is to assure my dear sister of my welfare and increasing confidence in the success of my undertaking.

A WORD FROM THE GRAVE

Dear reader, when you have looked deep into the pale, watery eyes of my monstrous creation, then you will have known fear.

So read on – if you dare. On the left, you will see the story unfold, and on the right, you can learn about the search for eternal youth, the awesome power of lightning, the workings of the mind, and the creation of a terrifying, hideous monster.

My discoveries went with me to the grave, but one day, science may give humans the power to create another monster. If so, I hope they learn from my story. Finally, please remember that Frankenstein is *my* name, not the name of my monster!

Yours,

Mary Shelley

Frankenstein was written by Mary Shelley in 1816, when she was just eighteen years old. The story resulted from a game among Mary and her friends, who were on vacation near Geneva, Switzerland.

As the weather was stormy, the friends warmed themselves by a blazing log fire, telling tales of the supernatural. Each agreed to write a story in "playful imitation" of the old ghost stories. Mary was the only one to finish, excited by her awful nightmares. And what a story it is!

During the month of June, Walton set sail to begin his search for the pole. Fair winds swept his ship safely past the giant icebergs of the northern seas, and his heart beat faster with each passing day. But Walton felt terribly alone – not one of his crew seemed to share his dream.

Two months into the voyage, and hundreds of miles from port, a thick fog descended. Overnight, a sea of ice closed in around the ship, leaving no escape from its icy jaws. By midday, however, the fog began to clear, revealing an astonishing sight. A gigantic human figure drove a dog sled at great speed over the ice. It swept past the ship, then disappeared into the distance. How could this be, so far from land?

The next day, the sailors found another dog sled, its occupant almost frozen to death. He was quickly brought on board, but for days lay weak and silent.

Finally, struggling to speak, the stranger whispered, "I am Victor Frankenstein, and before I die, I must tell you how I came to be in this terrible place..."

Archa

St. Petersburg

RUSS

Orkney
Islands

NORWAY

SWEDEN

IRELAND

ENGLAND

POLAND

GERMAN
STATES

Ingolstadt

AUSTRIA-
HUNGARY

FRANCE

SWITZERLAND

Geneva Montanvert

OTTOMAN
EMPIRE
(TURKEY)

ITALIAN STATES

SPAIN

MYTHS OF THE NORTH

In Mary Shelley's time, very little was known about the true hazards facing polar explorers. So, when Walton set off for the North Pole (*right*), he was embarking on a voyage to a mysterious, mythical place that remained undiscovered until over a century later.

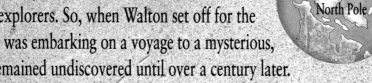

North Pole

Chilled Out!

The first attempt to visit the North Pole was by hot-air balloon in 1797, but the three Swedish travelers had to abandon their craft (*left*). Two of them were found years later, frozen to death. In 1909, Robert Peary (*right*) and Matthew Henson supposedly were the first to reach the pole by land. Some experts say they could not have walked so far in such a short time. The first team to prove (using scientific instruments) that they had reached their target on land, was led by Ralph Plaisted, in 1968. They had traveled on snowmobiles!

Legends of the Pole

Until Peary's journey in 1909, there was fierce scientific argument about what was at the North Pole. Scientists worked out from the spinning of the Earth that the sun never sets in summer. Perhaps the pole was a warm paradise, like the garden of Eden? The force of magnetism was also little understood, and myths grew about the pole as a magical place. In Edgar Rice Burroughs' story, *The Land That Time Forgot*, it was inhabited by giant, prehistoric monsters (*left*)!

Victor told Walton of his happy childhood in Geneva with his caring father and mother. When he was four years old, his parents adopted a baby girl, who became his greatly loved sister, Elizabeth.

As a young boy, Victor thirsted for knowledge, and became obsessed with the search for the secrets of heaven and earth. Deep into the night he would read the works of the alchemists, who aimed to turn iron into gold and to discover the secret of eternal youth. At school, he became best friends with a fellow student, Henry Clerval.

One night, a huge thunderstorm erupted in the sky. Victor watched from the door of the family house, wondering at the violence of the storm. He saw a huge lightning bolt snake through the sky toward the ground, where it struck an oak tree in the yard. This awesome display of electrical power convinced him that he was wasting his time on the alchemists. He was 15 years old.

From now on, he would study the secrets of electricity and the physical world.

ALCHEMY!

The tradition of alchemy goes back 2,000 years to Ancient Greece and Egypt. It began with the Greek philosopher Aristotle, who believed that one substance could be changed into another by altering its mixture of the four basic elements – earth, air, fire, and water.

Gold and Potions

Z_e

zinc

Alchemists prepared chemicals from many sources, such as animals, plants, and rocks (*above*), and mixed and heated them together. They worked with metals (see alchemic symbols, *left*), strong acids, and choking gases. They hoped to discover the "philosopher's stone," a chemical which would turn inexpensive metals like iron into gold, and the elixir of youth, a potion that would let you live forever.

lead

The Alchemists – The Early Chemists

Though some alchemists were fake, others helped develop the science of chemistry. In the story, Victor read books by the medieval alchemists Albertus Magnus, who wrote about and dissected many plants and animals, and Paracelsus (*right*), who studied plants and prescribed mineral drugs for his patients. However, Paracelsus also believed in gnomes!

In his later years, even the English mathematician Isaac Newton (1642 - 1727) turned to alchemy. But in the late 18th century, Antoine Lavoisier founded the modern science of chemistry, and alchemy was forgotten.

When Victor turned 17, his parents decided he should go to Ingolstadt University in Germany. But on the day of his departure, his adopted sister Elizabeth caught scarlet fever. Nursed by his mother, she recovered. But his mother contracted the disease herself, and passed away. Victor was heartbroken. "Why are those dear to us taken away," he cried. "Is there no way to bring them back?"

After his mother's funeral, Victor left for Ingolstadt. He took an instant dislike to Krempe, his professor of natural philosophy, who hated the alchemists and called their work "nonsense." Krempe was also a squat and ugly man, and this annoyed Victor. He much preferred his professor of chemistry, Waldman, who was pleasant and kind looking. "The old alchemists may have proved nothing," Waldman said, "but they showed the way to the heavens, penetrating the tiniest recesses of nature in their quest for knowledge."

Victor was fascinated by these comments, and as he lay awake one night, he vowed to make the ultimate discovery, life itself!

THE QUEST FOR LIFE

Mary Shelley would have heard of many advances in what we now call life sciences, and she refers to some of these in *Frankenstein*. For example, in the 1650s, Anton van Leeuwenhoek, a Dutchman, had made many discoveries with early microscopes, and began to study individual living cells – "the tiniest recesses of nature" that Waldman talked about.

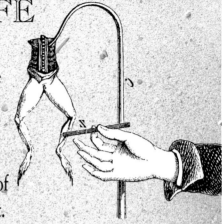

The Living Flame

It was only in the 1770s that English scientist Joseph Priestley and French "Father of Chemistry" Antoine Lavoisier (*left*) discovered that air contains oxygen. They found that a living body breathes in and uses oxygen in the same way a burning flame does.

An Unseen Power!

Scientists before Shelley's time were familiar with electricity, but only in the form we call static electricity (see page 15). In the 1780s, Italian professor Luigi Galvani was dissecting dead animals when their legs jumped as though alive (*top*). Galvani thought that "animal electricity" came from their bodies.

Rival Alessandro Volta argued that electricity was in fact made by a combination of chemicals in their bodies and the metal dissection tools. In 1800, Volta (from whose name we get "volt") produced a flowing electrical current – by chemical means using a pile of metal and salted cardboard disks (*right*).

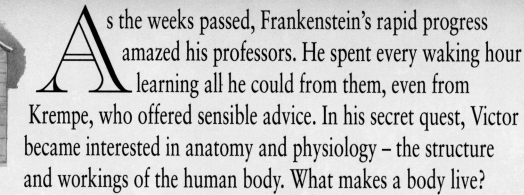

As the weeks passed, Frankenstein's rapid progress amazed his professors. He spent every waking hour learning all he could from them, even from Krempe, who offered sensible advice. In his secret quest, Victor became interested in anatomy and physiology – the structure and workings of the human body. What makes a body live?

To solve the mysteries of life, Frankenstein first studied death. In the dead of night, he visited lonely graveyards and dug up bodies, to see how the flesh rotted away and was consumed by worms. Despite his horror with this work, Victor drove himself on, neglecting his friends, his appearance, and his health.

It was in a sudden and brilliant flash of genius that Victor finally realized the secret of life and how to make it. "But," said Frankenstein as he told his story to Walton, "I cannot reveal the secret of life. When I have finished, you will know why."

MAKING A MONSTER

Frankenstein used corpses to help him learn about the body. But in the Middle Ages, people were prevented from dissecting human corpses, for religious reasons. Anyway, what was the point? Such study could not help medicine, since people believed their fate lay in God's hands.

Anatomy Comes of Age

This blind acceptance was not good enough for the scientists of the Renaissance. In 1543, Andreas Vesalius published his work *De Humani Corporis Fabrica*, which contained drawings of muscles, nerves, and other body parts in beautiful detail. A professor at Padua in Italy, Vesalius made his drawings (*see modern color version, above*) from dissected corpses, some of which he had stolen! Scientists also began to do experiments on living animals – and people. By the 1620s, English physician William Harvey had shown that the heart pumps, or circulates, blood around the body (*left*). This organ is vital and central for life.

Any Spare Bodies?

Many bodies for dissection came from grave robbing, digging up corpses from their coffins. In the 1820s in Edinburgh, Scotland, William Burke and William Hare (*right*) even murdered people, then sold their corpses for research!

Driven by obsession, Frankenstein began to build a human body, to which he would give the gift of life. He knew that many body parts were small and difficult to work on. So he decided to make his creation eight feet tall, as this meant he could work with larger parts. Now when he visited graveyards, he didn't just look at bodies, he sawed parts off them! Returning with the bloody bags to his attic room, he worked all night, as though in a feverish trance.

For two years, Frankenstein slaved away, his room piled high with strange devices and chemicals. Little by little, he perfected his methods, piece by piece, his creation took shape.

One stormy November night, at one o'clock in the morning, the rain beat against the attic window, and the lightning flashed above.

Frankenstein looked at the huge body, his body tingling with anticipation. Finally, he was ready to do something that only God had done before – create life...

ELECTRIC MAGIC

In the early 19th century, electricity was all the rage as traveling showmen gave hair-raising displays of shocks and sparks using electrostatic generators. So perhaps electricity was in Mary Shelley's mind when she wrote about Victor Frankenstein's experiments.

The Electrical Fluid

In the 1740s, American scientist Benjamin Franklin experimented with static electricity. This was thought

to be a liquid like water, but unseen – the "electrical fluid." Franklin had the idea that a lightning bolt might be electricity, like a huge spark. He flew a kite in a thunderstorm (*above*) and showed that an electric charge traveled down the damp string. It was a very dangerous act and he was lucky to survive.

Later generators, such as that invented by Van de Graaff in the 1930s (*left*), can create charges of over a million volts, making massive sparks. Small machines have been used by filmmakers to add atmosphere to Frankenstein's laboratory!

Animal Electricity

Electricity has long existed in the animal world, too. There are electric rays (*right*), eels, and catfish. They make pulses of electricity with special muscle blocks, as a type of "radar" for navigating in muddy waters, and to shock and stun their prey. So Galvani (page 11) was partly right, after all!

The thunder burst with a terrific crash, and a bolt of lightning struck the roof. Rain and wind swept the attic, blowing out the candles and knocking Victor to the ground. In the darkness, something stirred. The lightning flashed again – and Victor stared into the eyes of his breathing, moving creation. Then, at the moment of his great triumph, he came to his senses.

He had tried to make the monster beautiful, but looking now, he found it to be repulsive. Filled with horror, he ran away to hide in his room. Eventually, he slumped into restless sleep, dreaming terrible nightmares about the monster, his sister Elizabeth, his dead mother, and slithering worms.

He awoke to see the monster standing there, grinning and holding out its hand. Frankenstein escaped and ran as fast as he could. After a night wandering the streets, he returned to the attic, to find his friend Henry Clerval outside. Frankenstein opened the door. The monster was gone...!

THE MONSTER

In Frankenstein movies, we usually see the monster being shocked into life by bolts of lightning, amid great sparks, dials, and metal globes. Mary Shelley's book has none of this. Victor says only, "I collected the instruments of life around me, that I might infuse a spark of being into the lifeless thing that lay at my feet." The rest has been added by filmmakers!

The Clumsy Giant

The monster's appearance differs, too. In most Frankenstein movies, he is clumsy, walks with a shuffling waddle, and has two bolts through the neck. These features first appeared in the classic 1931 *Frankenstein (below)*. However, this was influenced more by the monster in an earlier film, *The Golem* (1927, *above*), than by the monster in the book. In some films, Victor even gives the monster the brain of a brilliant criminal!

Will the Real Monster Step Forward?

In the book, Shelley's monster is well-proportioned and powerful, with long black hair and pearly white teeth. However, these desirable features contrast with a yellow, flaky skin that hardly covers the muscles and blood vessels beneath. Ugh! The monster should also have dull, yellow, watery eyes in pale sockets, and straight black lips.

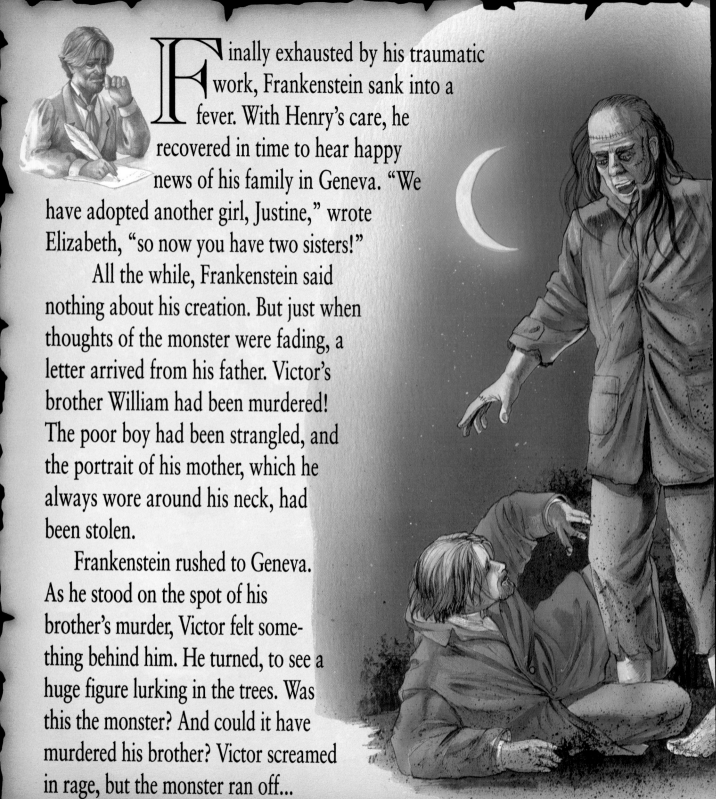

Finally exhausted by his traumatic work, Frankenstein sank into a fever. With Henry's care, he recovered in time to hear happy news of his family in Geneva. "We have adopted another girl, Justine," wrote Elizabeth, "so now you have two sisters!"

All the while, Frankenstein said nothing about his creation. But just when thoughts of the monster were fading, a letter arrived from his father. Victor's brother William had been murdered! The poor boy had been strangled, and the portrait of his mother, which he always wore around his neck, had been stolen.

Frankenstein rushed to Geneva. As he stood on the spot of his brother's murder, Victor felt something behind him. He turned, to see a huge figure lurking in the trees. Was this the monster? And could it have murdered his brother? Victor screamed in rage, but the monster ran off...

MAN-MADE BEASTS

When Mary Shelley created her ghastly monster, she was following in a long tradition of stories about man-made people:

◉ According to historical legend, the medieval German alchemist Albertus Magnus built a robot that answered questions. In the 16th century, the alchemist Paracelsus, was rumored to have devised a formula for creating life!

◉ In 1580, Rabbi Low of Prague made a human figure from river mud and brought it to life using magic (*above*). Though golems were meant to be servants (like robots), Low's golem terrorized the folk of Prague.

◉ The oldest story is from *The Epic of Gilgamesh*, a poem written 4,000 years ago. It tells of a wild monster, Enkidu (*right*), made from clay to provide a companion for the lonely hero Gilgamesh. Like Frankenstein's monster, Enkidu lived among the wild animals before learning to speak and live like a human (*below*).

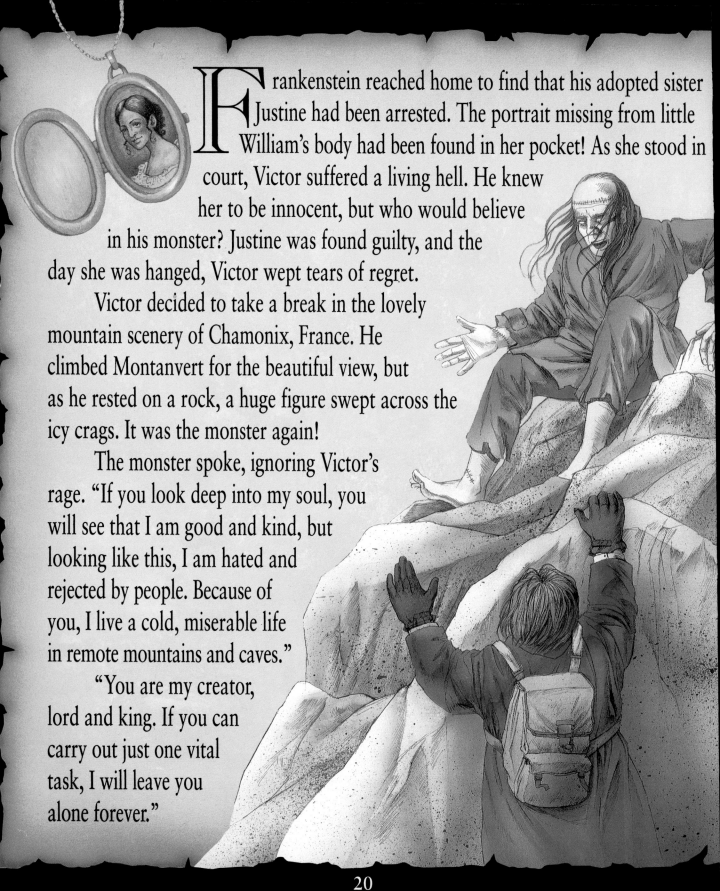

Frankenstein reached home to find that his adopted sister Justine had been arrested. The portrait missing from little William's body had been found in her pocket! As she stood in court, Victor suffered a living hell. He knew her to be innocent, but who would believe in his monster? Justine was found guilty, and the day she was hanged, Victor wept tears of regret.

Victor decided to take a break in the lovely mountain scenery of Chamonix, France. He climbed Montanvert for the beautiful view, but as he rested on a rock, a huge figure swept across the icy crags. It was the monster again!

The monster spoke, ignoring Victor's rage. "If you look deep into my soul, you will see that I am good and kind, but looking like this, I am hated and rejected by people. Because of you, I live a cold, miserable life in remote mountains and caves."

"You are my creator, lord and king. If you can carry out just one vital task, I will leave you alone forever."

PLAYING WITH FIRE

When Victor's brother is strangled by the monster, Mary Shelley wanted to show that when you have godlike powers, and create living beings, things will go terribly wrong! The full title of her book is *Frankenstein, or The Modern Prometheus*, because in Greek legend, Prometheus was horribly punished for creating humans.

Never-Ending Agony

Prometheus shaped clay and water – perhaps his own tears – into the shape of a human. Then Goddess Athena breathed life and soul into the shape. Zeus was furious that the giant Prometheus should help create humans and then teach them the secret of fire (*right*). He chained the giant to a rock, and an eagle pecked out his liver each day! As Prometheus was immortal, the liver grew back each night, so the torture never ended.

A Warning of Evil

Still angry, Zeus sent Pandora to Earth, to bring evil upon the world. When she married Prometheus' brother, Epimetheus, they were given a mysterious jar. Pandora knew not to open it, but being curious, she lifted the lid. Countless evils leapt out and troubled the world ever after. So like Prometheus, will Victor bring evil upon the world?

"But first, hear my tale," said the monster. "After you created me, I lived wild in the forests near Ingolstadt. I learned to eat and drink, and identify trees and animals. But whenever I approached a village, people drove me away. My only refuge was the outhouse of a cottage."

"Through a hole in the wall I could see and hear a man, Felix, his aged father, and a young woman called Safie. She had come from Turkey, so Felix taught her the local language and customs and told her about history, society, and good and evil. As she learned, so did I. I found some old books and taught myself to read. Watching Felix and Safie, I also learned what love is.

"Among the books was a Bible, and I read how God made Adam – the perfect man. But when I looked at my face in the water, I thought my creator must be the devil himself!"

"When I fled from your laboratory, I took a coat and later, I found your notes in the pocket. I knew then," said the monster, "that you were my father, who made me so hideous that even you could not bear to look at me!"

CREATION!

Reading a Bible, Frankenstein's monster learns about the Christian story of God creating Adam and Eve (*right*). However, just about every culture has its own stories about how humans were formed.

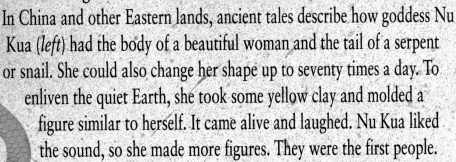

An Amazing Snake!

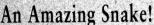

In China and other Eastern lands, ancient tales describe how goddess Nu Kua (*left*) had the body of a beautiful woman and the tail of a serpent or snail. She could also change her shape up to seventy times a day. To enliven the quiet Earth, she took some yellow clay and molded a figure similar to herself. It came alive and laughed. Nu Kua liked the sound, so she made more figures. They were the first people.

In time, Nu Kua became tired. She took a vine, dipped it into the yellow clay, and flicked lumps from it. These also came alive. They were poor people, while those she had molded with her hands were rich people.

Khnum the Creator

In ancient Egypt, Khnum was the Lord of Destiny. He had a ram's head and a man's body. Khnum was thought to be the maker of all things, and he made the first people from clay on a potter's wheel (*right*). Indeed, he was kept very busy, for some people believed that he molded the body of every baby ever born!

"I approached the old man in the cottage. He was blind, so he spoke kindly to me. But when Felix and the others returned, they saw my foul appearance. They beat me with sticks, and for the first time, feelings of hatred filled my heart. I waited until they had gone for a walk, then set fire to the straw I had gathered. In minutes, the cottage was engulfed in flames. I danced in joy as it burned to the ground.

"I learned from your notes that you lived in Geneva. On the way there, I saw a young girl slip and fall into a fast-flowing river. I rescued her, but the only reward I got was a gunshot wound. Nursing my injury, I swore revenge on all mankind. "

"I came to Geneva to search for my maker. I hoped that a young child might accept my appearance, but as I came near a boy, he screamed that his father, Mr. Frankenstein, would rescue him. I knew this child must be your relative, and saw an opportunity to get my revenge. In a blind fury, I grabbed his throat and lifted him off the ground. He wriggled in agony, but my powerful hands squeezed the life from his helpless body."

SPARE PARTS

Could we build a living creature, like Victor does in the story? Today, doctors can transplant even complicated organs like the heart, and some scientists predict that one day we might even transplant the human brain. But such medical advances are a long way from creating something just from parts.

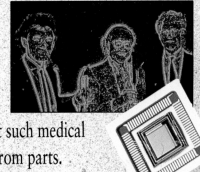

Bionic Organs

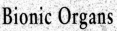

As well as creating artificial joints (*left*) and plastic blood vessels, scientists are now using electronics to replace some of the body's most complex organs. An eye-sized miniature video camera detects patterns of light and turns them into electrical signals, which are processed by a silicon chip (*above*) and passed on to the brain.

Artificial hands have also been designed where electronic sensors detect nerve signals from the skin of the wearer, to control electric-motor muscles. Sensors in the bionic fingers give the wearer feedback about touch and grip.

Transplants

A transplant involves taking a body part from one (sometimes dead) person and putting it into another person. Many different organs can be transplanted, such as the heart (1), kidneys (2), lungs (3), and liver (4). Such operations save many lives, so Victor Frankenstein's act of creation has come half true!

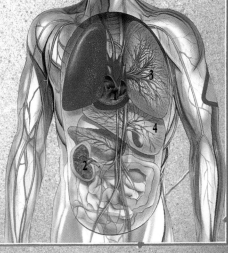

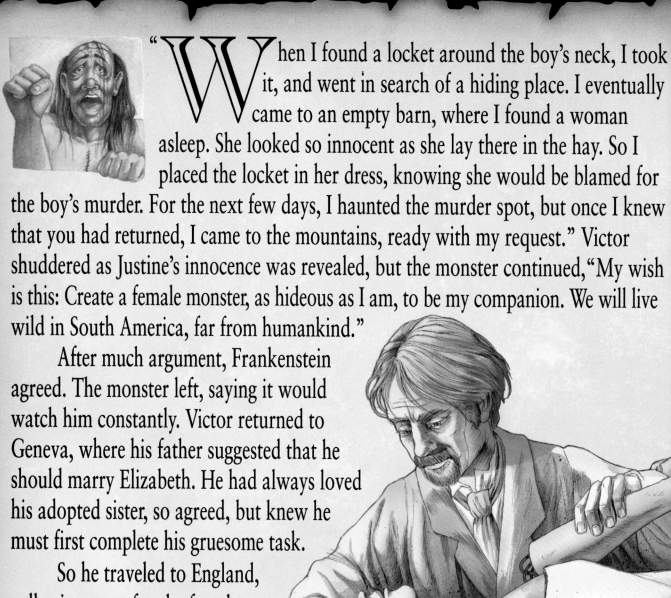

"When I found a locket around the boy's neck, I took it, and went in search of a hiding place. I eventually came to an empty barn, where I found a woman asleep. She looked so innocent as she lay there in the hay. So I placed the locket in her dress, knowing she would be blamed for the boy's murder. For the next few days, I haunted the murder spot, but once I knew that you had returned, I came to the mountains, ready with my request." Victor shuddered as Justine's innocence was revealed, but the monster continued, "My wish is this: Create a female monster, as hideous as I am, to be my companion. We will live wild in South America, far from humankind."

After much argument, Frankenstein agreed. The monster left, saying it would watch him constantly. Victor returned to Geneva, where his father suggested that he should marry Elizabeth. He had always loved his adopted sister, so agreed, but knew he must first complete his gruesome task.

So he traveled to England, collecting parts for the female monster – an arm here, a leg there. Then, heading north, he rented a cottage on the remote Orkney islands. But his nightmare had only just begun…

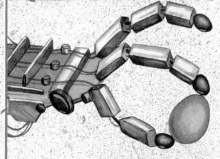

CLEVER DEVILS

Mary Shelley's monster is capable of thinking deeply, learning fast, and showing emotions such as sadness and joy. Its devious mind even plants the locket on Justine to put the blame on her. But if we were making a monster from robot parts today, would it be clever enough to do anything more than simple, routine tasks like painting cars?

Lessons From Life

Billions of dollars worldwide are spent on AI (Artificial Intelligence) projects. One area of development is neural networks. Electronic circuits (*below left*) and input-output devices try to mimic the workings of the living nerve cells, or neurons (*above left*), in an animal's brain and nervous system. These nerve cells develop complex, ever-changing connections, as the animal learns and remembers.

Artificial Stupidity!

Researchers are producing mobile robots like Genghis (*below*), that "think" in a very basic way. Genghis uses heat sensors and pressure-sensitive  "whiskers" to detect and follow objects, and electronic circuits to make decisions and control its actions. Genghis isn't very clever compared to humans, but the research may help to develop robots that can find their way into a maze of machinery, search for faults, and fix them.

Frankenstein sweated through days and nights, slicing and stitching the parts that would form the female monster. But his blood ran cold at the thought of this new creation. Would it agree to be the partner of the male monster? If the pair went to South America, could they start a new breed that would destroy humankind?

As Frankenstein sat in his laboratory, he sensed that someone was watching. He looked up, and his eyes met the ghastly face of the monster, pressed against the window. Trembling with passion, Victor ripped apart the half-finished monster. Frankenstein had broken his promise – and the monster would be alone forever. With a blood-curdling howl, it smashed the cottage door with a single blow. Terrified but resolute, Victor refused to continue his task. "If that is your decision," said the monster, "so be it. But remember, I shall be with you on your wedding night."

The next day, Victor got a note from Henry, asking to meet him in Scotland. He set off in his boat, and far from land, threw the female monster's remains into the sea.

EXOTIC ROBOTICS

In the 19th century, there were no robots as we know them. Otherwise, Mary Shelley might have considered a monster made from pieces of machinery. But even today's most sophisticated machines look crude next to the fine workings of the human body.

From Automatons to Robots

The most robotlike objects of Mary Shelley's time were mechanical toys known as automatons, operated by internal gears and levers. The word "robot" (meaning worker) was invented later, in 1921, by Czech writer Karel Capek. Some robots are designed to look like humans, like Manny (*above*), but most are built for specific tasks.

Robot Marvels!

There are some very specialized robots around today. Cleo (*above*) is a thumbsized robot surgeon, designed to work inside the human intestine. It is either steered by a remote-control joystick or it can move on its own. A tiny claw takes tissue samples for lab analysis, then Cleo leaves through the same exit from which we excrete food! NASA has designed Dante to climb down steep slopes into the inferno of a volcano. It takes samples of rocks in places where a human would fry in seconds. One day, a robot may explore volcanoes on Mars.

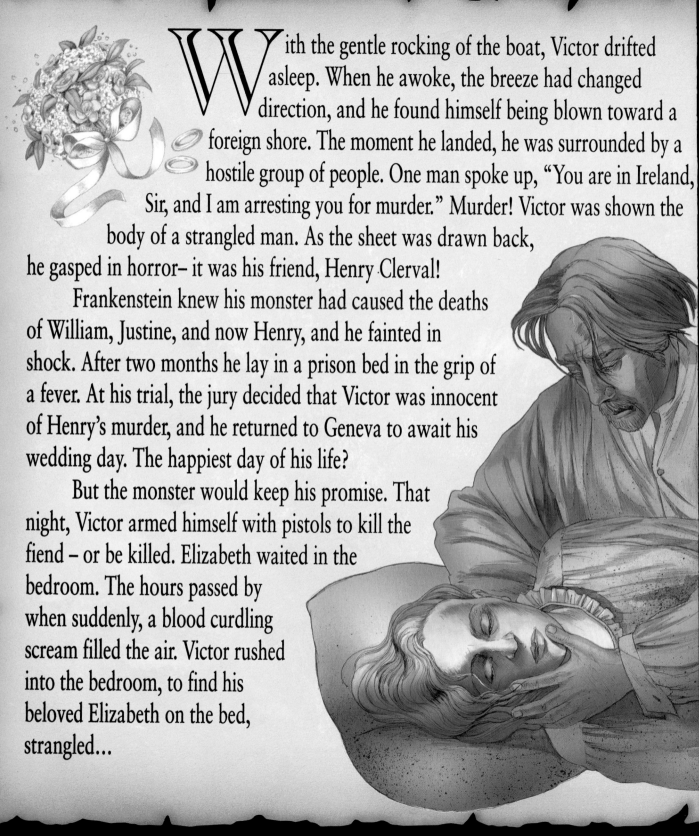

With the gentle rocking of the boat, Victor drifted asleep. When he awoke, the breeze had changed direction, and he found himself being blown toward a foreign shore. The moment he landed, he was surrounded by a hostile group of people. One man spoke up, "You are in Ireland, Sir, and I am arresting you for murder." Murder! Victor was shown the body of a strangled man. As the sheet was drawn back, he gasped in horror– it was his friend, Henry Clerval!

Frankenstein knew his monster had caused the deaths of William, Justine, and now Henry, and he fainted in shock. After two months he lay in a prison bed in the grip of a fever. At his trial, the jury decided that Victor was innocent of Henry's murder, and he returned to Geneva to await his wedding day. The happiest day of his life?

But the monster would keep his promise. That night, Victor armed himself with pistols to kill the fiend – or be killed. Elizabeth waited in the bedroom. The hours passed by when suddenly, a blood curdling scream filled the air. Victor rushed into the bedroom, to find his beloved Elizabeth on the bed, strangled...

GENETIC MONSTERS

Forty years after *Frankenstein* was written, Gregor Mendel discovered the basic laws of heredity – how features are passed from parents to their offspring. For example, in humans, we say that hair color "runs in the family." In 1953, James Watson and Francis Crick discovered that DNA (*right*) carried genes, in the form of a genetic code. Today, genetics is used to create new forms of life!

Genetic Lookalikes!

Genetic fingerprinting looks at the DNA in a sample of a living thing, such as a drop of blood. The results show as patterns of dark bands in a clear gel (*below*). They can locate the source from which the samples came, as each person's DNA is unique (except twins). But scientists will soon be able to create clones (identical copies). Would you like to meet a clone of yourself?

New Forms of Life

In the film *Jurassic Park*, genes from blood sucked by a 160 million-year-old mosquito (*top*) are used to recreate dinosaurs. Though this is very unlikely, scientists are already using genetic engineering (mixing genes) to create new plants and animals, such as crops with bigger, juicier fruit (*above*). Some people, however, are worried that such methods might be used to create a monstrous breed of humans!

Frankenstein looked up from his dead wife, to see the monster's grinning face at the window, its once sad features twisted into a mask of evil. Victor fired his pistol, but the shot whistled past the monster's ear. The beast raced away, laughing as it went, and plunged into the lake.

The sound of the pistol brought servants rushing to Victor's side, but the monster had vanished. The news of Elizabeth's death proved too much for the weak heart of Victor's father, and he died a few days later. Though Victor's heart was broken, one thought ruled his mind – death to the monster!

The next day, he visited the graves of his murdered family – and there was the hideous ogre, challenging him to follow. The chase had begun.

Victor pursued the creature from the Rhône to the Mediterranean, from the Black Sea to Russia. All the while, it taunted him with messages left on trees, leading him to the icy north. There he would feel the cold, hunger, and loneliness it had endured.

THE ORIGINS OF LIFE

Even with today's knowledge, it is difficult to imagine how Frankenstein could have created a living creature. Ancient Greeks such as Aristotle (*right*) believed that living things could arise from non-living matter, with the addition of a special life force. Otherwise, how did maggots (*left*) grow in meat, when you could not see them before? This theory was known as spontaneous generation.

Too Tiny To See

From the early 1600s, the invention of the microscope opened up a new world too small for the unaided eye. Patient studies revealed that maggots in meat hatched from small eggs, laid there by flies. The idea of spontaneous generation was finally halted by biologist Louis Pasteur (*right*) in the 1860s. He revealed that nourishing soup did not go bad because germs appeared in it spontaneously. The germs had landed in it from the air!

Once Upon A Time

In 1953, Stanley Miller and Harold Urey recreated in a flask the conditions on Earth four billion years ago (*left*). There was heat and gases like the ancient volcanoes, plenty of chemicals like the ancient oceans, and sparks of electricity like lightning. The experiment created amino acids, the building blocks of living matter! So Victor could have created life from just chemicals, after all!

The final message left by the monster included these words: "Prepare! Wrap yourself in furs, for we shall soon enter upon a journey where your sufferings will satisfy my eternal hatred." A few weeks later, having obtained a sled and dogs, Frankenstein reached a small town on the northern shore of Russia. The night before his arrival, a gigantic monster had terrified the local people, stolen food, and headed out to the ice-covered ocean. Frankenstein followed it for three weeks, consumed with rage. He even sighted the monster, but the ice broke up, and he became stranded on a small iceberg.

"Now that you have heard my story," said Frankenstein to Walton, "swear to me that you will seek out the monster and kill him." At that moment, the first mate ran into the cabin, his face a picture of fear. "Captain, if the ice does break, for all our sakes, forget your quest to find the North Pole, and sail south instead." But Walton simply replied, "Never..."

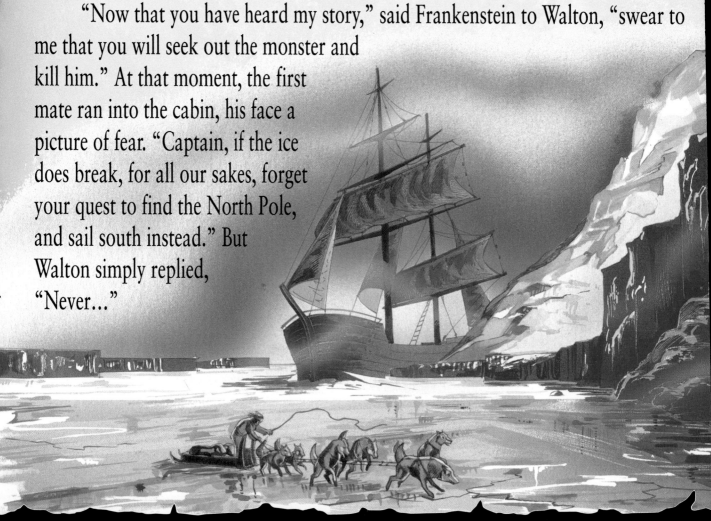

MOVIETIME FRANKENSTEIN

If you read Mary Shelley's original *Frankenstein*, you may be surprised at how different it is from the many movie versions produced over the years. Next time you get to see one of the films, see if you can spot some of the changes to the story:

👁 The introduction of the character Igor, the hunchbacked assistant of Victor Frankenstein. He is usually weird and sinister, but was portrayed as a comic fool by Marty Feldman (*left*) in *Young Frankenstein* (1974).

👁 The scene in which local people band together to attack the monster with sticks and stones, to encourage sympathy for the poor creature (*below left*).

👁 In the book, the monster is created in an attic room. For a big-budget movie, a large, looming castle is often thought to be more exciting!

👁 In *Bride of Frankenstein* (1935, *below center*) and Kenneth Branagh's *Frankenstein* (1994, *below right*), Victor actually makes a female companion for his monster, but both monsters come to a nasty end!

As the days passed, Frankenstein became weaker and weaker. The ice held tight, and the crew again asked that the ship turn south. This time, Frankenstein answered, "Are you so easily turned from your glorious expedition? Be steady to your purposes and firm as a rock. Return as heroes who have fought and conquered, and who do not know what it is to turn their backs on the foe." Frankenstein spoke with such passion that the crew was silenced. But Walton had learned from Frankenstein the evils that obsession could bring, and gave in to the crew's demands.

The next evening, after clinging to life for many days, Victor Frankenstein died. Walton had listened to his incredible story – and believed it. Later that night, as he wrote to his sister Margaret, Walton heard what sounded like a human voice in Victor's cabin.

When he entered the cabin, he saw a huge figure crouched over Victor's body – the monster!

UGLY MUGS!

In the story, Frankenstein's monster only becomes evil because people hate it for being ugly. But many of today's horror films assume that if anything is horrible-looking, it must be bad. A few, however, take a more interesting look at ugliness:

Robots Have Feelings, Too!

In the *Terminator* movies, a robot in a living person is played by Arnold Schwarzenegger (*above*). In the first film he is a cold killer, but in the sequel his artificial intelligence helps him to learn about human feelings.

As in *Frankenstein*, we gradually come to understand the monster's situation. Our hatred and loathing for it turn into sympathy and even warmth. In *Robocop* (*right*), the bionic parts are on the outside, and it is easy to feel pity for the man inside.

Love is Blind?

In the comedy *The Man with Two Brains*, scientist Steve Martin (*left*) falls in love with a woman who only exists as a speaking brain in a jar! More horrible is *The Fly*, where a scientist accidentally mixes his genes with those of a fly (*right*). But his girlfriend still cares for the man trapped in the fly's body!

The monster looked at Walton, paused, then turned again toward the lifeless form of its creator, weeping tears of remorse and guilt. Seeing this, fear gave way to anger in Walton's heart: "How dare you weep, when it wa you who killed Frankenstein."

"I have never had sympathy from any man," replied the monster, "and I do not expect it from you. But it was only my loneliness that drove me to kill the lovely and the helpless. How could Victor marry Elizabeth, yet not give me the same happiness b making a partner for me. But fear not, for I shall leave your vessel and seek the farthest northern point of the world, build a funeral fire, and burn in agony for my terrible sins."

Then the giant being sprang from the cabin window onto an iceberg near the vessel, and was swept away into the darkness by the icy currents.

MONSTER TALK

Alchemy – The chemistry of the Middle Ages, which was mostly concerned with turning cheap metals into gold and finding the secret of eternal youth.

Anatomy – The dissection of the body to discover where each part goes and what it does.

Artificial Intelligence – Making computers think like humans, e.g. learning, and making decisions.

Bionics – Replacing parts of the body with electronic/mechanical parts, such as power-controlled limbs.

DNA – A molecule that contains all the genetic information (like hair color) passed on from parents to offspring. It stands for deoxyribonucleic acid. Phew!

Genes – A gene is a portion of DNA that controls one feature, like eye color.

Neuron – A cell found in the brain which passes messages along the nervous system.

North Pole – The *geographical* North Pole is the most northern point on the globe. This is different from the *magnetic* North Pole, which is further south and to which compass needles point.

Robotics – The technology of designing, building, and using robots (mechanical beings).

Spontaneous generation – The ancient theory that life can arise from materials that are not alive, with the help of a special life force. This has been proved false by modern science.

Transplant – A procedure in which a body part is removed from one person and put into another person.

INDEX

Photocredits   *Abbreviations: t – top, m – middle, b – bottom, r – right, l – left.* 5l, 9 both, 11 both, 15t, 21, 23 both, 33m, 34: Mary Evans Picture Library; 5r, 17 both, 35bl, 35bm: Universal (Courtesy Kobal Collection); 6, 25t, 31t, 32, 35br, 36, 37m: Frank Spooner Pictures; 7: Amicus (Courtesy Kobal); 8, 33tr: Hulton Deutsch; 13 both, 15m, 25m, 27 all, 29t, 31b, 38: Science Photo Library; 14, 15b: Bruce Coleman Ltd; 16: Tristar/ American Zoetrope (Courtesy Kobal); 19b: Ancient Art & Architecture Collection; 28, 33tl: Roger Vlitos; 29b, NASA; 35t, 37bl: 20th Century Fox (Courtesy Kobal); 37t: Carolco (Courtesy Kobal); 37br: Warner Bros (Courtesy Kobal); 39: Hammer (Courtesy Kobal).